Guide to Jakarta EE

Practical Guide

V. Telman

Practical Guide

1.Introduction

Jakarta EE (Enterprise Edition) is a platform for developing enterprise applications based on the Java programming language. It provides a standard set of specifications, APIs (Application Programming Interfaces), and tools that enable developers to create scalable, secure, and portable applications across various server environments. Jakarta EE, the successor to Java EE (Java Platform, Enterprise Edition), supports the development of complex applications, such as business management systems, e-commerce solutions, and backend services for distributed applications.

The primary advantage of Jakarta EE lies in its ability to abstract the complexity of enterprise application development by providing developers with ready-to-use tools for transaction management, security, data persistence, and network service connectivity. Jakarta EE is designed to be modular and composable, allowing developers to select only the necessary modules for their project, keeping the system agile and optimized.

History and Evolution of Jakarta EE

Jakarta EE has a history spanning over two decades, and its evolution is closely tied to the growth and success of Java as a programming language. Originally, the platform was known as Java EE, and before that as J2EE (Java 2 Platform, Enterprise Edition).

- **J2EE (Java 2 Platform, Enterprise Edition)**: Launched in 1999 by Sun Microsystems, J2EE was a response to the growing demand for web-based enterprise applications. J2EE provided a set of APIs for developing distributed applications and addressed complex issues such as transaction management, security, and database connectivity. Key technologies included Servlets, JavaServer Pages (JSP), and Enterprise JavaBeans (EJB).

- **Java EE**: In 2006, with version 5, J2EE was renamed Java EE, and it saw increased standardization and simplification of the programming model. Java EE specifications were expanded, including modern technologies such as JAX-RS for RESTful services and significant improvements to persistence APIs (JPA).

- **Transition to Jakarta EE**: In 2017, Oracle, which had acquired Sun Microsystems, donated the Java EE project to the Eclipse Foundation, paving the way for the creation of a more dynamic and innovative open-source project. This marked the transition to Jakarta EE, with version 8 released in 2019. The main initial difference between Java EE 8 and Jakarta EE 8 was in branding and governance, as the APIs were identical. However, Jakarta EE 9 was a turning point, featuring a significant migration of packages from `javax.*` to `jakarta.*`.

Jakarta EE continues to evolve under the guidance of the Eclipse Foundation, rapidly adapting to emerging technologies such as cloud computing, microservices, and container architectures.

Key Features

Jakarta EE is distinguished by several features that make it a powerful and versatile platform for enterprise application development:

1. **Portability**: Applications developed with Jakarta EE can run on various application servers that support Jakarta EE specifications, ensuring code portability.

2. **Transaction Management**: Jakarta EE simplifies transaction management by providing an automated infrastructure to ensure data integrity across distributed transactions.

3. **Security**: It offers tools for application-

level security management, including authentication, authorization, and encryption, in compliance with industry standards.

4. **Web Services Support**: It includes specifications for creating and managing SOAP (JAX-WS) and REST (JAX-RS) web services, facilitating easy integration with other applications and distributed services.

5. **Modular Components**: Jakarta EE is based on a modular architecture. Developers can choose only the necessary components, reducing application overhead.

6. **Standardization**: The platform is governed by standardized specifications, ensuring interoperability between different vendors and high code quality.

Comparison with Java EE

Jakarta EE can be seen as the natural evolution of Java EE, but there are some key differences worth noting:

1. **Namespace**: The most significant difference between Jakarta EE and Java EE is the change in namespace from `javax.*` to `jakarta.*`. This change was required for legal reasons after Oracle donated Java EE to the Eclipse Foundation.

2. **Governance and Development**: While Java EE was under Oracle's control, Jakarta EE is now managed by the Eclipse Foundation, an open-source organization that allows for greater flexibility and a more active and open community. This has led to faster development cycles and greater innovation.

3. **Modernization**: Jakarta EE is geared towards adopting modern technologies such as microservices, cloud computing, and integration with container architectures, fostering compatibility with cloud-native

environments and the use of containers like Docker and Kubernetes.

Jakarta EE Architecture

The architecture of Jakarta EE is designed to support the development of distributed, modular, and scalable applications. It follows a multi-tier architecture, where application processing and logic are separated into different layers to ensure greater flexibility and maintainability.

Fundamental Concepts of Jakarta EE Architecture

1. **Multi-tier Architecture**: Jakarta EE architecture consists of distinct layers:

   - **Client Tier**: This layer includes the user interface and can be a web page, a desktop application, or a mobile app.

   - **Web Tier**: Responsible for handling

HTTP requests. Key technologies include Servlets, JSP, and Facelets (JSF).

- **Business Logic Tier**: Manages application logic and includes components like Enterprise JavaBeans (EJB) or CDI (Contexts and Dependency Injection).

- **Persistence Tier**: Houses technologies for data persistence management, such as JPA (Java Persistence API).

- **Enterprise Information Systems (EIS) Tier**: Connects the application to databases, messaging systems, and other enterprise resources.

2. **Server Independence**: A Jakarta EE application can run on any application server that supports Jakarta EE specifications, ensuring vendor independence.

3. **Modularity**: The architecture supports the use of independent modules, such as web modules (WAR), enterprise modules (EAR), and class libraries (JAR), promoting code isolation and maintainability.

Main Components and Modules

- **Servlets**: Servlets are server-side components that handle HTTP requests. They form the basis of web request handling in Jakarta EE.

- **JavaServer Pages (JSP)**: JSP is a technology that allows the creation of dynamic web pages with Java embedded in HTML.

- **JavaServer Faces (JSF)**: A framework for creating component-based user interfaces, which separates presentation logic from business logic.

- **Enterprise JavaBeans (EJB)**: EJB is a specification for managing server-side components that execute business logic in a secure, scalable, and transactional manner.

- **Java Persistence API (JPA)**: JPA is a specification for managing data persistence using Java objects mapped to relational databases.

- **Contexts and Dependency Injection (CDI)**: CDI provides a flexible infrastructure for dependency injection, managing component lifecycle, and facilitating interaction between components.

- **Java API for RESTful Web Services (JAX-RS)**: JAX-RS is a specification for creating RESTful services in a simple and standardized way.

Programming Model

Jakarta EE adopts a component-based programming model, which divides the application into modular and highly reusable units. Developers primarily work with annotations and XML configuration files, avoiding boilerplate code. CDI specifications play a central role in Jakarta EE's programming model, enabling dependency injection management between various components.

Development Environment Configuration

To develop Jakarta EE applications, configuring an appropriate development environment is necessary. Below are the software and hardware requirements along with the steps to set up the environment.

Software and Hardware Requirements

1. **Operating System**: Jakarta EE is cross-platform and can be used on Windows, Linux, or macOS.

2. **RAM**: At least 8 GB of RAM for smooth development, especially when using IDEs and application servers.

3. **Disk Space**: At least 10 GB of available space for development tools, application servers, and required libraries.

4. **Processor**: A multi-core processor is recommended to handle multiple processes concurrently during application compilation and execution.

Installing a Compatible JDK

The first step to start developing with Jakarta EE is to install a compatible version of the JDK (Java Development Kit). Jakarta EE 9 and later versions require at least **JDK 11**, but it is preferable to install the latest stable version of Java to ensure the best performance and updated support.

1. Download the JDK from the official Oracle website or from open-source providers such as AdoptOpenJDK.

2. Set up the `JAVA_HOME` environment variable and update the `PATH` to include the

JDK binary.

3. Verify the installation by running the command `java -version`.

Choosing an Application Server

To run Jakarta EE applications, you need to use a compatible application server. Some of the most popular options include:

1. **Payara**: A derivative of GlassFish, Payara is known for its stability and focus on enterprise applications. It is an excellent choice for production environments.

2. **WildFly**: A lightweight, highly configurable, and open-source server. WildFly offers great integration with modern microservice architectures.

3. **TomEE**: Based on Apache Tomcat, TomEE extends the popular web container with Jakarta EE support, making it a lightweight solution for Java EE/Jakarta EE applications.

Recommended Development Tools (IDEs)

An integrated development environment (IDE) is crucial for boosting developer productivity. The best IDEs for Jakarta EE development include:

1. **Eclipse IDE**: An open-source IDE, particularly integrated with Jakarta EE due to its connection to the Eclipse Foundation. It offers plugins to simplify enterprise application development.

2. **IntelliJ IDEA**: With built-in support for Java EE and Jakarta EE, IntelliJ IDEA is one of the most powerful IDEs, featuring advanced tools for refactoring and debugging.

3. **NetBeans**: Originally developed by Sun Microsystems, NetBeans is an open-source IDE with excellent support for Java EE and Jakarta EE, including support for servers like GlassFish.

Jakarta EE represents the future of enterprise development in Java, constantly evolving to meet the needs of modern applications

. With its modular architecture, well-defined specifications, and strong open-source community support, Jakarta EE continues to be a leading platform for large-scale enterprise applications.

2.Jakarta EE Application Development

Jakarta EE is a robust and flexible platform that enables the development of scalable and modular enterprise applications. Developing a Jakarta EE application involves several steps, from project setup to managing the lifecycle of the components and services that make up the application. In this detailed guide, we will explore all the stages of creating a Jakarta EE application, starting with an overview of the application lifecycle, moving to basic project setup, and then managing dependencies using `pom.xml` for Maven.

Overview of the Jakarta EE Application Lifecycle

A Jakarta EE application follows a well-defined lifecycle, involving various architecture components such as Servlets, EJB (Enterprise JavaBeans), JPA (Java Persistence API) resources, and more. The lifecycle of an enterprise application can be divided into several phases:

1. **Deployment**: The application is deployed on a Jakarta EE-compliant application server (such as Payara, WildFly, or TomEE). During this phase, the application server analyzes configuration files (like `web.xml` or `persistence.xml`), manages dependencies, and allocates necessary resources (such as database connections or network resources).

2. **Initialization**: Once deployed, the application performs initialization operations. For example, Servlets are initialized through the `init()` method, while EJB beans can be initialized with dependency injection through CDI (Contexts and Dependency Injection).

3. **Execution**: During the application's normal operation, user requests are routed to the server, which invokes the appropriate components. Servlets handle HTTP requests, EJB beans manage business logic, and JPA resources interact with the database.

4. **State Management**: Jakarta EE provides mechanisms for managing session state and transactions, such as HTTP sessions and distributed transactions. Sessions can be persistent or transient, depending on the application's needs.

5. **Shutdown and Resource Release**: When the application is deactivated or redeployed, Jakarta EE performs a cleanup cycle, releasing allocated resources (such as database connections or objects in memory). This includes closing active sessions and releasing unfinished transactions.

Creating a Basic Project

Creating a basic Jakarta EE project involves several essential steps, such as selecting the IDE, configuring Maven, creating core components like Servlets or EJB, and integrating a database with JPA. We will use Maven to manage dependencies and structure the project.

Step 1: Setting Up the Development Environment

Before starting, make sure you have the following tools installed:

- **Java Development Kit (JDK)**: Version 11 or later.

- **Apache Maven**: A build tool that simplifies dependency management.

- **An IDE**: I recommend **IntelliJ IDEA**, **Eclipse IDE**, or **NetBeans**.

Step 2: Creating the Project with Maven

To create a new Jakarta EE project with Maven, open a console or terminal and use the Maven `archetype:generate` command. This command allows you to create a basic project with the typical structure of a Jakarta EE web application.

```bash
mvn archetype:generate
-DgroupId=com.example
-DartifactId=jakartaee-app
-DarchetypeArtifactId=maven-archetype-
webapp -DinteractiveMode=false
```

- `groupId`: Defines the main package of the project, typically in reversed domain format (e.g., `com.example`).

- `artifactId`: Is the name of the project or module, in this case, `jakartaee-app`.

- `maven-archetype-webapp`: Creates a basic structure for a Java EE/Jakarta EE web application.

After running the command, Maven generates the project structure, which will look something like this:

```
```

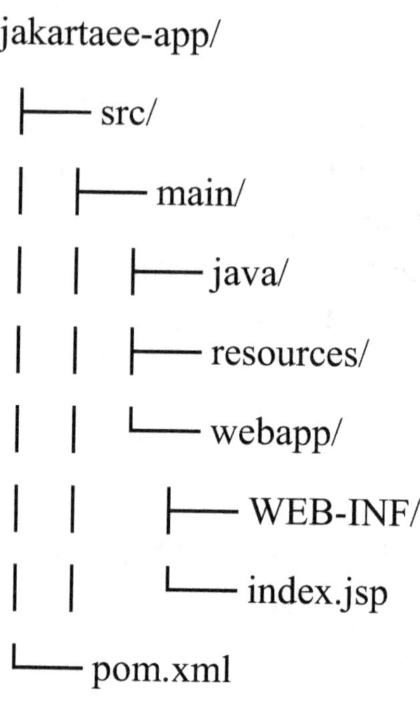

```
jakartaee-app/
├── src/
│   ├── main/
│   │   ├── java/
│   │   ├── resources/
│   │   └── webapp/
│   │       ├── WEB-INF/
│   │       └── index.jsp
└── pom.xml
```

Step 3: Configuring the `pom.xml` File for Maven

The `pom.xml` file is the heart of every Maven project. It contains project information such as dependencies, build plugins, and other configurations essential for managing and deploying the project. For a Jakarta EE project, the `pom.xml` must include dependencies for the Jakarta EE specifications, as well as any necessary libraries for the technologies you'll use (such as JPA for persistence or JAX-RS for RESTful services).

Here’s an example `pom.xml` for a basic Jakarta EE project:

```xml
<project
xmlns="http://maven.apache.org/POM/4.0.0"

xmlns:xsi="http://www.w3.org/2001/XMLSc
hema-instance"

xsi:schemaLocation="http://maven.apache.org
/POM/4.0.0 http://maven.apache.org/maven-
v4_0_0.xsd">
    <modelVersion>4.0.0</modelVersion>


    <!-- Project identifier -->
    <groupId>com.example</groupId>
```

```
    <artifactId>jakartaee-app</artifactId>
    <version>1.0-SNAPSHOT</version>
    <packaging>war</packaging>

    <name>Jakarta EE App</name>
    <description>Basic Jakarta EE project</description>

    <!-- Define the minimum JDK version -->
    <properties>
<maven.compiler.source>11</maven.compiler.source>
<maven.compiler.target>11</maven.compiler.target>
<failOnMissingWebXml>false</failOnMissingWebXml>
    </properties>
```

```
<!-- Main dependencies -->
<dependencies>
    <!-- Jakarta EE API -->
    <dependency>
        <groupId>jakarta.platform</groupId>
        <artifactId>jakarta.jakartaee-
api</artifactId>
        <version>10.0.0</version>
        <scope>provided</scope>
    </dependency>

    <!-- Library for unit testing -->
    <dependency>
        <groupId>junit</groupId>
        <artifactId>junit</artifactId>
        <version>4.13.2</version>
        <scope>test</scope>
    </dependency>
```

```
    </dependencies>


    <!-- Build plugin configuration -->
    <build>
        <finalName>jakartaee-app</finalName>
        <plugins>
            <!-- Plugin for compiling the Java
project -->
            <plugin>

<groupId>org.apache.maven.plugins</groupI
d>
                <artifactId>maven-compiler-
plugin</artifactId>
                <version>3.8.1</version>
                <configuration>
                    <source>11</source>
                    <target>11</target>
                </configuration>
            </plugin>
```

```
    </plugins>
  </build>
</project>
```

Explanation of `pom.xml`

1. **GroupId and ArtifactId**: The `groupId` represents the organization or group developing the project, in this case, `com.example`. The `artifactId` represents the unique project name, here `jakartaee-app`.

2. **Version**: `version` indicates the project's version (`1.0-SNAPSHOT`, which denotes a development version).

3. **Packaging**: `war` (Web Application Archive) is the packaging type. For a Jakarta EE web application, the packaging is always `war`, as it will be deployed on an application server.

4. **Compiler Properties**: Specifies the version of Java to use for the project. In this case, the project is set to use Java 11.

5. **Dependencies**:

- The main dependency here is `jakarta.jakartaee-api`, which provides all the Jakarta EE APIs (such as Servlet, EJB, JPA, and CDI). The `scope` is set to `provided`, as the Jakarta EE application server will provide these libraries at runtime.

- The `junit` dependency is included for unit testing.

6. **Build and Plugins**:

- The `maven-compiler-plugin` is configured to compile the project with Java 11.

- The `finalName` specifies the name of the WAR file generated in the `target` folder during the build phase.

Step 4: Creating Jakarta EE Components

Now that the project is set up, you can start creating Jakarta EE components, such as Servlets, EJBs, or JPA Entities.

Servlet Example

A Servlet is a Java class that handles HTTP requests and generates responses. Let's create a simple Servlet that responds with "Hello, Jakarta EE!".

1. Create a new Servlet class in the directory `src/main/java/com/example/servlets`:

```java
package com.example.servlets;

import jakarta.servlet.ServletException;
import jakarta.servlet.annotation.WebServlet;
```

```
import jakarta.servlet.http.HttpServlet;

import jakarta.servlet.http.HttpServletRequest;

import
jakarta.servlet.http.HttpServletResponse;

import java.io.IOException;


@WebServlet("/hello")

public class HelloServlet extends HttpServlet
{

   @Override

   protected void doGet(HttpServletRequest
request, HttpServletResponse response)
throws ServletException, IOException {

       response.setContentType("text/html");

       response.getWriter().println("<h1>Hello,
Jakarta EE!</h1>");

   }

}
```

2. The Servlet is mapped to the `/hello` URL using the `@WebServlet("/hello")` annotation. When a user visits the URL, the `doGet()` method is invoked, and the Servlet responds with "Hello, Jakarta EE!".

Step 5: Running the Application

To run the application, you can use one of the Jakarta EE-compliant application servers, such as Payara or WildFly.

1. **Deploying the Application on Payara**:

   - Ensure Payara Server is running.

   - Copy the generated WAR file to the deployment folder of Payara (`$PAYARA_HOME/glassfish/dom

ains/domain1/autodeploy`).

   - Access `http://localhost:8080/jakartaee-app/hello` to see the Servlet's message.

3.Guide to Servlets, JavaServer Faces (JSF), and JAX-RS in Jakarta EE

Jakarta EE is a robust development platform for enterprise applications, offering a wide range of technologies for building web applications and RESTful services. Among these technologies, **Servlet**, **JavaServer Faces (JSF)**, and **JAX-RS** are key components. In this detailed guide, we will explore each technology thoroughly, with practical examples to demonstrate how to develop applications using each of these APIs.

Servlets in Jakarta EE

Introduction to Servlets

Servlets are a fundamental component of Jakarta EE and serve as server-side Java classes capable of handling HTTP requests and generating dynamic responses. Servlets are the entry point for web applications and allow direct interaction with HTTP protocols (GET, POST, PUT, DELETE, etc.).

Servlets have been part of the Java stack for many years and have become even more powerful with Jakarta EE through integration with other APIs and enterprise components. They are used to handle requests such as form submissions, database interactions, session management, and more.

Creating a Servlet

Creating a servlet in Jakarta EE is straightforward. A servlet is defined as a Java class that extends `HttpServlet` and overrides the `doGet()` or `doPost()` methods to handle requests.

Here's an example of a servlet that responds to an HTTP GET request with a welcome message:

```java
package com.example.servlets;


import jakarta.servlet.ServletException;
import jakarta.servlet.annotation.WebServlet;
import jakarta.servlet.http.HttpServlet;
import jakarta.servlet.http.HttpServletRequest;
import jakarta.servlet.http.HttpServletResponse;
import java.io.IOException;


@WebServlet("/hello")
public class HelloServlet extends HttpServlet {


    @Override
    protected void doGet(HttpServletRequest request, HttpServletResponse response) throws ServletException, IOException {
```

```
        response.setContentType("text/html");

response.getWriter().println("<h1>Welcome to Jakarta EE Servlet!</h1>");

    }

}
```

- `@WebServlet("/hello")`: This annotation maps the servlet to the URL `/hello`. When a user accesses this URL, the servlet is invoked.

- `doGet()`: This method is called when an HTTP GET request is received. It generates a simple HTML response.

Handling Requests and Responses

Servlets handle client (HTTP) requests and generate server responses. Requests contain information such as URLs, parameters, headers, and input data, while responses are constructed to include HTML, JSON, or other data formats.

To handle HTTP POST requests, you can override the `doPost()` method.

```java
@Override
protected void doPost(HttpServletRequest request, HttpServletResponse response) throws ServletException, IOException {
    String name = request.getParameter("name");
    response.setContentType("text/html");
    response.getWriter().println("<h1>Hello, " + name + "!</h1>");
}
```

In this example, the `name` parameter is extracted from the request and used to customize the response.

Configuring Servlets in `web.xml`

Although the `@WebServlet` annotation is the most common way to configure a servlet, it is also possible to do so via the `web.xml` configuration file, useful for more complex or legacy projects.

Here's an example of servlet configuration in `web.xml`:

```xml
<web-app
xmlns="http://java.sun.com/xml/ns/javaee"

xmlns:xsi="http://www.w3.org/2001/XMLSchema-instance"

xsi:schemaLocation="http://java.sun.com/xml/ns/javaee
```

```
        http://java.sun.com/xml/ns/javaee/web-app_3_0.xsd"
        version="3.0">


    <servlet>
        <servlet-name>HelloServlet</servlet-name>
        <servlet-class>com.example.servlets.HelloServlet</servlet-class>
    </servlet>


    <servlet-mapping>
        <servlet-name>HelloServlet</servlet-name>
        <url-pattern>/hello</url-pattern>
    </servlet-mapping>


</web-app>
```

In this case, the servlet is manually configured to be accessible through the URL `/hello`.

JavaServer Faces (JSF)

Overview of JSF

JavaServer Faces (JSF) is a server-side framework for building web user interfaces in Jakarta EE. JSF uses a component-based model that allows the development of dynamic web pages based on XHTML, with a lifecycle that handles input conversion and validation, binding to managed beans, and navigation between pages.

JSF simplifies the management of interactions between the user interface and business logic by providing a declarative mechanism to define views and link them to the backend.

Creating a Simple JSF Application

To create a JSF application, you need to configure an XHTML page that represents the view and a **managed bean** that handles the business logic.

Here’s a simple JSF page (`index.xhtml`):

```xml
<html
xmlns="http://www.w3.org/1999/xhtml"
    xmlns:h="http://xmlns.jcp.org/jsf/html">
<h:head>
   <title>JSF Example</title>
</h:head>
<h:body>
   <h:form>
      <h:outputLabel for="name" value="Enter
your name: " />
```

```
      <h:inputText id="name"
value="#{helloBean.name}" />

      <h:commandButton value="Say Hello"
action="#{helloBean.sayHello}" />

      <h:outputText
value="#{helloBean.greeting}" />

   </h:form>

</h:body>

</html>
```

This XHTML page uses JSF tags to create a form that submits a name to a bean and displays a greeting message. The binding between the view and the bean is done using EL expressions (`#{}`).

Managing Views and Beans

Managed beans in JSF are simple Java classes that handle the state and logic of the user interface. Here's an example of `HelloBean`:

```java
package com.example.jsf;

import
jakarta.enterprise.context.RequestScoped;
import jakarta.inject.Named;

@Named
@RequestScoped
public class HelloBean {
    private String name;
    private String greeting;

    public String getName() {
        return name;
    }
```

```
  public void setName(String name) {
    this.name = name;
  }

  public String getGreeting() {
    return greeting;
  }

  public void setGreeting(String greeting) {
    this.greeting = greeting;
  }

  public void sayHello() {
    this.greeting = "Hello, " + this.name +
"!";
  }
}
```

```

- `@Named`: The annotation makes the bean accessible in the view under the name `helloBean`.

- `@RequestScoped`: Indicates that the bean has a lifecycle limited to the current HTTP request.

### Integrating XHTML and CSS

JSF supports separation between logic and presentation, making it easy to integrate CSS to improve the appearance of pages. For example, you could add a custom CSS file in `index.xhtml` as follows:

```xml
<h:head>
    <title>JSF Example</title>
    <h:outputStylesheet name="styles.css" />
```
```

```
</h:head>
```

The `styles.css` file could contain styles to customize the appearance of the input fields and button:

```css
input[type="text"] {
   padding: 5px;
   font-size: 14px;
}

button {
   background-color: #4CAF50;
   color: white;
   padding: 10px 20px;
   border: none;
   cursor: pointer;
```

}

```

## JAX-RS (Java API for RESTful Web Services)

### Introduction to JAX-RS

**JAX-RS** is the standard API in Jakarta EE for creating RESTful web services. REST (Representational State Transfer) is an architecture that leverages HTTP methods to build services that can be consumed by various clients (web, mobile, desktop).

With JAX-RS, you can easily create a REST API by mapping resources to URLs and defining methods that respond to various HTTP methods (GET, POST, PUT, DELETE).
```

Creating REST Services with JAX-RS

Here’s an example of a simple REST service with JAX-RS:

```java
package com.example.rest;

import jakarta.ws.rs.GET;
import jakarta.ws.rs.Path;
import jakarta.ws.rs.Produces;
import jakarta.ws.rs.core.MediaType;

@Path("/hello")
public class HelloResource {

    @GET
    @Produces(MediaType.TEXT_PLAIN)
```

```
    public String sayHello() {
        return "Hello, JAX-RS!";
    }
}
```

- `@Path("/hello")`: Indicates that the resource is accessible at the URL `/hello`.

- `@GET`: Indicates that this method handles HTTP GET requests.

- `@Produces(MediaType.TEXT_PLAIN)`: Specifies that the response will be in plain text.

Handling Parameters and Responses

JAX-RS supports extracting parameters from the HTTP request using annotations such as `@QueryParam`, `@PathParam`, and `@HeaderParam`. Here's an example of handling a query parameter:

```java
@GET
@Path("/greet")
@Produces(MediaType.TEXT_PLAIN)
public String greet(@QueryParam("name") String name) {
    return "Hello, " + name + "!";
}
```

In this case, the `name` parameter is extracted from the URL and used in the response. For example, accessing `/greet?name=John` will return "Hello, John!".

Error Handling in REST APIs

Error handling is crucial for ensuring that REST APIs provide clear feedback to clients.

JAX-RS offers the **Response** concept to customize error messages.

Here's an example of error handling:

```java
@GET
@Path("/greet")
@Produces(MediaType.TEXT_PLAIN)
public

 Response greet(@QueryParam("name") String name) {
    if (name == null || name.isEmpty()) {
        return Response.status(Response.Status.BAD_REQUEST)
                       .entity("Name parameter is missing")
                       .build();
```

```
    }

    return Response.ok("Hello, " + name +
"!").build();

}
```

In this example, if the `name` parameter is missing, a 400 error with an appropriate message is returned.

In this guide, we have explored three key technologies in Jakarta EE: **Servlets**, **JavaServer Faces (JSF)**, and **JAX-RS**. Each technology offers a unique set of tools for developing modern and scalable web applications. Servlets handle basic HTTP requests, JSF provides a powerful framework for managing user interfaces, and JAX-RS makes creating RESTful APIs quick and flexible.

Together, these technologies form a solid foundation for developing complex and modular enterprise applications in Jakarta EE.

4.Guide to Java Persistence API (JPA) and Enterprise JavaBeans (EJB) in Jakarta EE

Jakarta EE is a comprehensive platform for developing enterprise applications, offering a wide range of tools for handling persistence, transactions, security, and more. Two key components used in this platform for persistence and business logic management are the **Java Persistence API (JPA)** and **Enterprise JavaBeans (EJB)**.

In this detailed guide, we will explore:

1. **Java Persistence API (JPA)**:

   - What JPA is and how it works

   - Persistence configuration

   - CRUD operations with JPA

   - Entity relationships and transaction management

2. **Enterprise JavaBeans (EJB)**:

   - Introduction to EJB

   - Types of EJB: Managed Beans, Session Beans, and Message-Driven Beans

   - Dependency injection with CDI (Contexts and Dependency Injection)

   - Transactions and concurrency management

Java Persistence API (JPA)

What JPA is and how it works

JPA (Java Persistence API) is a standard API for managing persistence and mapping Java entities to relational data stores (like databases). Its main function is to provide a standardized way to interact with databases without having to write SQL queries directly. With JPA, data in database tables is mapped to Java objects known as **entities**, and vice versa.

At the heart of JPA is the concept of the **Entity Manager**, which manages the lifecycle of entities and provides an interface to perform persistence operations such as saving, updating, and deleting data.

Persistence configuration

To use JPA in a Jakarta EE application, you need to configure a persistence unit, which defines the database connections and the entity classes that will be mapped. This configuration is usually found in an XML file called `persistence.xml`, located in the `META-INF` folder.

Here’s an example of a `persistence.xml` file:

```xml
```

```
<persistence
xmlns="http://xmlns.jcp.org/xml/ns/persistenc
e"

xmlns:xsi="http://www.w3.org/2001/XMLSc
hema-instance"

xsi:schemaLocation="http://xmlns.jcp.org/xml
/ns/persistence

http://xmlns.jcp.org/xml/ns/persistence/persist
ence_2_2.xsd"
         version="2.2">


   <persistence-unit
name="MyPersistenceUnit" transaction-
type="JTA">
      <jta-data-
source>jdbc/myDataSource</jta-data-source>

<class>com.example.entities.User</class>
      <properties>
         <property
```

```
name="jakarta.persistence.jdbc.url"
value="jdbc:mysql://localhost:3306/mydb"/>

        <property
name="jakarta.persistence.jdbc.user"
value="root"/>

        <property
name="jakarta.persistence.jdbc.password"
value="password"/>

        <property
name="jakarta.persistence.jdbc.driver"
value="com.mysql.cj.jdbc.Driver"/>

      </properties>

   </persistence-unit>


</persistence>
```

In this example:

- **persistence-unit**: Defines a persistence unit that includes the database configuration and the classes managed by JPA.

- **jta-data-source**: Refers to a data source configured in the container, used for transactions managed by JTA (Java Transaction API).

- **properties**: Includes details for database connection, such as URL, username, password, and JDBC driver.

CRUD operations with JPA

JPA simplifies **CRUD** (Create, Read, Update, Delete) operations on entities mapped to database tables. Each operation can be performed using the Entity Manager provided by JPA.

1. **Create**

To create a new record in the database, you need to persist a new entity using the `persist()` method of the Entity Manager.

```java
@Entity
public class User {
    @Id
    @GeneratedValue(strategy = GenerationType.IDENTITY)
    private Long id;
    private String name;
    private String email;

    // Getters and setters...
}
```

```java
public void createUser(EntityManager em) {
    User user = new User();
```

    user.setName("John Doe");

    user.setEmail("john@example.com");

    em.getTransaction().begin();

    em.persist(user);

    em.getTransaction().commit();

}

```

In this example, a new `User` object is created and persisted in the database.

#### 2. **Read**

To read data from the database, you can use the `find()` method of the Entity Manager to retrieve an entity by its identifier.

```java

public User findUser(EntityManager em,

Long id) {
    return em.find(User.class, id);
}
```

Or you can execute a JPQL (Java Persistence Query Language) query to retrieve entities based on custom criteria.

```java
public List<User>
findAllUsers(EntityManager em) {
    return em.createQuery("SELECT u FROM
User u", User.class).getResultList();
}
```

3. **Update**
```

To update an existing entity, simply modify the fields of the retrieved entity, and the entity manager will synchronize the changes with the database.

```java
public void updateUser(EntityManager em, Long id, String newName) {
    User user = em.find(User.class, id);
    em.getTransaction().begin();
    user.setName(newName);
    em.getTransaction().commit();
}
```

4. **Delete**

To delete an entity, you need to use the `remove()` method of the Entity Manager.

```java
public void deleteUser(EntityManager em, Long id) {
    User user = em.find(User.class, id);
    em.getTransaction().begin();
    em.remove(user);
    em.getTransaction().commit();
}
```

Entity relationships and transaction management

JPA supports various relationships between entities, such as **one-to-one**, **one-to-many**, **many-to-one**, and **many-to-many**. These relationships can be mapped using annotations like `@OneToOne`, `@OneToMany`, `@ManyToOne`, and `@ManyToMany`.

Example of a One-to-Many relationship

Suppose we have a relationship between `User` and `Order`, where a user can have multiple orders. This relationship can be mapped as follows:

```java
@Entity
public class User {
    @Id
    @GeneratedValue(strategy = GenerationType.IDENTITY)
    private Long id;
    private String name;

    @OneToMany(mappedBy = "user")
    private List<Order> orders = new ArrayList<>();
```

```
    // Getters and setters...
}

@Entity
public class Order {
    @Id
    @GeneratedValue(strategy = GenerationType.IDENTITY)
    private Long id;
    private String product;

    @ManyToOne
    @JoinColumn(name = "user_id")
    private User user;

    // Getters and setters...
}
```

In this example:

- `@OneToMany` in the `User` class indicates that a user can have multiple orders.

- `@ManyToOne` in the `Order` class indicates that an order belongs to a single user.

In Jakarta EE environments, JPA transactions can be automatically managed using JTA, where the container handles the entity manager and transaction synchronization.

Enterprise JavaBeans (EJB)

Introduction to EJB

Enterprise JavaBeans (EJB) is one of the

key technologies in Jakarta EE used to develop scalable, transactional, and secure enterprise components. EJBs are primarily used to encapsulate the business logic of enterprise applications and handle complex operations such as distributed transaction management, concurrency, and security.

EJBs provide three main types of beans:

1. **Session Beans**: Handle business logic and can be either stateful or stateless.

2. **Message-Driven Beans**: Respond to messages from queues or topics.

3. **Managed Beans**: Java components managed by the container.

Types of EJB: Managed Beans, Session Beans, and Message-Driven Beans

1. **Session Beans**

Session Beans are the most common type of beans in Jakarta EE. They manage interactions with the client and can be stateless or stateful.

- **Stateless Session Bean**: Do not maintain state between method calls. Each request is treated independently.

Here's an example of a Stateless Session Bean:

```java
import jakarta.ejb.Stateless;

@Stateless
public class UserService {

    public String greetUser(String name) {
        return "Hello, " + name + "!";
    }
```

}

```

- **Stateful Session Bean**: Maintain state between method calls, meaning client information is preserved throughout the session.

```java
import jakarta.ejb.Stateful;

@Stateful
public class ShoppingCart {

    private List<String> items = new ArrayList<>();

    public void addItem(String item) {
        items.add(item);

```
    }

    public List<String> getItems() {
        return items;
    }
}
```

2. **Message-Driven Bean (MDB)**

Message-Driven Beans (MDB) are used to process messages asynchronously, typically from a JMS (Java Message Service) messaging queue.

```java
import jakarta.ejb.MessageDriven;

import jakarta.jms.Message;

import jakarta.jms.MessageListener;
```

```
@MessageDriven
public class OrderProcessor implements MessageListener {

    @Override
    public void onMessage(Message message) {
        // Process the incoming message
    }
}
```

Dependency injection with CDI (Contexts and Dependency Injection)

CDI (Contexts and Dependency Injection) is a Jakarta EE specification that simplifies dependency injection in enterprise components, allowing for more modular and flexible code.

For example, you can use `@Inject` to inject an EJB into another component:

```java
import jakarta.inject.Inject;

public class OrderService {

    @Inject
    private PaymentService paymentService;

    public void processOrder(Order order) {
paymentService.processPayment(order.getPaymentDetails());
    }
}
```

```

### Transactions and

concurrency management

EJBs provide built-in support for transactions and concurrency. Transactions are managed using annotations like `@TransactionAttribute`, which defines how methods participate in transactions.

For example, you can specify that a method requires a new transaction:

```java
import jakarta.ejb.TransactionAttribute;

import jakarta.ejb.TransactionAttributeType;

@Stateless
```
```

```
public class PaymentService {

    @TransactionAttribute(TransactionAttributeType.REQUIRES_NEW)
    public void processPayment(PaymentDetails details) {
        // Process payment in a new transaction
    }
}
```

EJB also supports concurrency management, allowing developers to handle multiple simultaneous requests and ensure thread safety.

In this guide, we have explored the key features and use cases of **Java Persistence API (JPA)** and **Enterprise JavaBeans (EJB)** in Jakarta EE applications. JPA provides a robust framework for managing persistence, while EJBs encapsulate the business logic, transactions, and concurrency, making Jakarta EE a powerful platform for building scalable enterprise applications.

5.Guide to Jakarta Contexts and Dependency Injection (CDI) and Jakarta Messaging (JMS)

Jakarta EE offers a robust environment for developing complex enterprise applications. Two central technologies in the Jakarta EE platform are **Jakarta Contexts and Dependency Injection (CDI)** and **Jakarta Messaging (JMS)**. CDI facilitates the management of dependencies and application contexts, while JMS provides a mechanism for asynchronous communication through messaging.

In this guide, we will explore in detail:

1. **Jakarta Contexts and Dependency Injection (CDI)**

   - Basic CDI concepts

   - Creating and managing CDI beans

   - Dependency injection and scoping

- Interceptors and decorators

2. **Jakarta Messaging (JMS)**
   - Introduction to JMS
   - Configuration of queues and topics
   - Producing and consuming messages
   - Transaction management in the context of messaging

Jakarta Contexts and Dependency Injection (CDI)

Basic CDI Concepts

Jakarta Contexts and Dependency Injection (CDI) is a Jakarta EE specification that introduces a framework for dependency injection and context management, enabling the development of modular and maintainable applications. CDI allows developers to define, manage, and inject components (called **beans**) declaratively, facilitating integration between various components of the Jakarta EE platform.

CDI primarily operates through the concept of **dependency injection**, which allows the CDI container to manage the creation and lifecycle of objects, and **context management**, which associates beans with different execution contexts such as HTTP requests, sessions, or applications.

Main Features of CDI:

- **Dependency Injection**: Components can declare their dependencies, which are automatically injected by the container.

- **Scoping**: Defines the lifecycle of a bean (e.g., request, session, application).

- **Interceptors and Decorators**: Allow extending and customizing the behavior of beans.

- **Events and Observers**: Enable asynchronous communication between components via the event system.

Creating and Managing CDI Beans

A **CDI bean** is a Java class annotated to be managed by the CDI container. These beans can be defined with annotations like `@ApplicationScoped`, `@RequestScoped`, `@SessionScoped`, and others.

Here is an example of a simple CDI bean:

```java
import jakarta.enterprise.context.RequestScoped;

import jakarta.inject.Named;


@Named
```

```
@RequestScoped
public class GreetingService {

    public String greet(String name) {
        return "Hello, " + name + "!";
    }
}
```

In this example, the `GreetingService` bean is defined as **RequestScoped**, meaning it will have a lifecycle limited to the duration of the HTTP request.

CDI Bean Lifecycle

The lifecycle of a bean is determined by its scope. CDI supports various scopes:

- **@ApplicationScoped**: The bean lives for the entire duration of the application.

- **@SessionScoped**: The bean exists for the duration of the HTTP session.

- **@RequestScoped**: The bean lives for the duration of a single HTTP request.

- **@Dependent**: The bean's lifecycle depends on that of its client.

Dependency Injection and Scoping

Dependency injection in CDI is based on the `@Inject` annotation. You can inject dependencies into fields, constructors, or methods of a component.

Example of dependency injection:

```java

import jakarta.inject.Inject;
```

```
public class WelcomeController {

    @Inject
    private GreetingService greetingService;

    public String welcomeUser(String name) {
        return greetingService.greet(name);
    }
}
```

In this example, the `GreetingService` is injected into the `WelcomeController` without the controller needing to explicitly manage the creation of the service. The `@Inject` annotation tells the CDI container to provide an instance of the appropriate bean.

Scoping

The scope of a CDI bean determines its lifecycle. Here are some common scopes:

1. **@ApplicationScoped**: The bean exists for the entire duration of the application.

```java
@ApplicationScoped
public class AppConfig {
    // Application configuration
}
```

2. **@SessionScoped**: The bean exists for the duration of the user session.

```java
@SessionScoped
public class UserSession {
    private String userName;
```

```java
    // Getters and setters...
}
```

3. **@RequestScoped**: The bean lives only for the duration of a single HTTP request.

```java
@RequestScoped
public class RequestLogger {
    public void log(String message) {
        System.out.println("Log message: " + message);
    }
}
```

4. **@Dependent**: The bean's lifecycle is tied to that of its client.

```java
```

```
@Dependent
public class ShortLivedBean {
    // Bean with a dependent lifecycle
}
```

Interceptors and Decorators

Interceptors and **decorators** in CDI provide powerful mechanisms to extend the behavior of beans without directly modifying their code. Interceptors allow code to be executed before or after a method runs, while decorators allow additional behavior to be layered on top of existing bean methods.

Interceptors

Interceptors are defined using the `@Interceptor` annotation and are applied to methods using a custom annotation, such as

`@Logged`. Here's an example:

1. Define an annotation for interceptors:

```java
import jakarta.interceptor.InterceptorBinding;
import java.lang.annotation.ElementType;
import java.lang.annotation.Retention;
import java.lang.annotation.RetentionPolicy;
import java.lang.annotation.Target;

@InterceptorBinding
@Target({ ElementType.METHOD, ElementType.TYPE })
@Retention(RetentionPolicy.RUNTIME)
public @interface Logged {}
```

2. Define the interceptor:

```java
import jakarta.interceptor.AroundInvoke;
import jakarta.interceptor.Interceptor;
import jakarta.interceptor.InvocationContext;

@Logged
@Interceptor
public class LoggingInterceptor {

    @AroundInvoke
    public Object logMethod(InvocationContext context) throws Exception {
        System.out.println("Invoking method: " + context.getMethod().getName());
        return context.proceed();
    }
```

```
}
```

3. Apply the interceptor to a bean:

```java
@Logged
public class PaymentService {

    public void processPayment() {
        // Payment logic
    }
}
```

When the `processPayment()` method is invoked, the `LoggingInterceptor` will be executed before the method, printing a log message.

Decorators

Decorators allow you to layer additional behavior on top of a bean by implementing the bean's interface and delegating part of the behavior to the original implementation.

Example:

1. Define an interface:

```java
public interface OrderService {
    void placeOrder(String item);
}
```

2. Original implementation:

```java
import jakarta.enterprise.context.ApplicationScoped;

@ApplicationScoped
public class OrderServiceImpl implements OrderService {

    @Override
    public void placeOrder(String item) {
        System.out.println("Order placed for: " + item);
    }
}
```

3. Define the decorator:

```java
import jakarta.decorator.Decorator;
import jakarta.decorator.Delegate;
import jakarta.inject.Inject;

@Decorator
public class OrderServiceDecorator implements OrderService {

    @Inject
    @Delegate
    private OrderService orderService;

    @Override
    public void placeOrder(String item) {
        System.out.println("Logging order: " + item);
        orderService.placeOrder(item);
    }
```

}

```

In this example, the `OrderServiceDecorator` adds logging functionality to the `placeOrder()` method of the `OrderServiceImpl` bean.

---

## **Jakarta Messaging (JMS)**

### Introduction to JMS

**Jakarta Messaging (JMS)** is an API that enables asynchronous communication between enterprise applications using messaging. JMS implements both **point-to-point** (queues) and **pub/sub** (topics) messaging systems. Messages can be sent and received between producers and consumers
```

via queues and topics, which act as intermediaries.

JMS is primarily used in scenarios where decoupling between components is essential, such as in distributed applications requiring asynchronous processing.

Configuration of Queues and Topics

To send and receive messages, you need to configure queues or topics where messages are transmitted and received.

- **Queue**: Used in the **point-to-point** model. A message sent to a queue is received by only one consumer.

- **Topic**: Used in the **pub/sub** model. A message sent to a topic can be received by multiple subscribers.

Example Configuration:

1. **Define a queue** in an application server (e.g., WildFly or Payara):

```xml
<jms-destinations>
   <jms-queue name="OrderQueue">
      <entry name="java:/jms/queue/OrderQueue"/>
   </jms-queue>
</jms-destinations>
```

2. **Define a topic**:

```xml
<jms-destinations>
```

```xml
   <jms-topic name="NewsTopic">
      <entry
name="java:/jms/topic/NewsTopic"/>
   </jms-topic>
</jms-destinations>
```

Producing and Consuming Messages

To produce and consume messages in JMS, use **JMS Producer** and **JMS Consumer** objects.

Example of Message Production:

```java
import jakarta.annotation.Resource;
import jakarta.jms.JMSContext;
import jakarta.jms.Queue;
```

```
import jakarta.inject.Inject;

public class OrderSender {

    @Inject
    private JMSContext jmsContext;

    @Resource(lookup =
"java:/jms/queue/OrderQueue")
    private Queue orderQueue;

    public void sendOrder(String orderDetails)
{

jmsContext.createProducer().send(orderQueue
, orderDetails);
        System.out.println("Order sent: " +
orderDetails);
    }
```

}

```

In this example, `JMSContext` is used to create a

producer that sends a message to the queue named `OrderQueue`.

#### Example of Message Consumption:

```java
import jakarta.jms.Message;

import jakarta.jms.MessageListener;

public class OrderReceiver implements MessageListener {

    @Override
```
```

```
    public void onMessage(Message message)
{
        // Process the received message
        System.out.println("Order received: " +
message.getBody(String.class));
    }
}
```

Here, the `OrderReceiver` listens for incoming messages on the queue and processes them.

Transaction Management

JMS supports transactional message sending and receiving, which ensures that either all messages are processed successfully or none are processed, helping maintain data consistency.

You can manage transactions programmatically using the `JMSContext` or leverage **Java EE managed transactions** with annotations like `@Transactional`.

Example:

```java
import jakarta.transaction.Transactional;

public class PaymentService {

    @Transactional
    public void processPayment() {
        // Transactional logic
    }
}
```

In this case, the `processPayment()` method is executed within a transaction. If any exception occurs, the transaction is rolled back automatically.

Jakarta Contexts and Dependency Injection (CDI) and Jakarta Messaging (JMS) are powerful tools within the Jakarta EE platform that enhance the modularity, maintainability, and scalability of enterprise applications. With CDI, you can manage dependencies and application contexts effortlessly, while JMS enables asynchronous communication between components, ensuring decoupled architecture. Mastering these technologies will significantly improve your ability to develop sophisticated, robust applications.

6.Jakarta Security and Testing of Jakarta EE Applications

In this guide, we will explore two fundamental aspects of Jakarta EE application development: **Jakarta Security** and **Testing Jakarta EE Applications**. These two topics are crucial for ensuring the security and quality of software in enterprise applications.

Jakarta Security

Security Mechanisms in Jakarta EE

Jakarta Security is a Jakarta EE specification that provides mechanisms to protect applications from unauthorized access and ensure the integrity and confidentiality of data. Jakarta Security is based on a security model that includes authentication, authorization, role management, and security policies.

Key Components of Jakarta Security:

1. **Authentication**: Identifies users accessing the application.

2. **Authorization**: Controls user access to resources based on roles and permissions.

3. **Role Management**: Defines and manages user roles and associated permissions.

4. **Policy-Based Security**: Allows defining security policies based on specific criteria.

Authentication and Authorization

Authentication in Jakarta EE occurs through a user identification mechanism, such as login and password. After authentication, authorization is managed, which defines the user's rights and permissions.

Configuring Authentication

Authentication can be configured in various ways, but in Jakarta EE, it is common to use configurations in the `web.xml` file and the `@RolesAllowed` annotation.

1. **Basic Configuration in `web.xml`**:

```xml
<web-app
xmlns="http://xmlns.jcp.org/xml/ns/javaee"

xmlns:xsi="http://www.w3.org/2001/XMLSc
hema-instance"

xsi:schemaLocation="http://xmlns.jcp.org/xml
/ns/javaee

http://xmlns.jcp.org/xml/ns/javaee/web-
app_4_0.xsd"

        version="4.0">
```

```xml
<security-constraint>
    <web-resource-collection>
        <web-resource-name>Secure Area</web-resource-name>
        <url-pattern>/secure/*</url-pattern>
    </web-resource-collection>
    <auth-constraint>
        <role-name>admin</role-name>
    </auth-constraint>
</security-constraint>

<login-config>
    <auth-method>BASIC</auth-method>
    <realm-name>MyRealm</realm-name>
</login-config>

<security-role>
    <role-name>admin</role-name>
```

```
    </security-role>

  </web-app>
```

In this example, only users with the `admin` role can access resources under the `/secure/*` path.

2. **Using Annotations for Authorization**:

```java
   import jakarta.annotation.security.RolesAllowed;
   import jakarta.ejb.Stateless;

   @Stateless
   public class SecureService {
```

```
    @RolesAllowed("admin")
    public void performAdminTask() {
        // Method accessible only to users with the 'admin' role
    }
}
```

In this example, the `performAdminTask` method is accessible only to users with the `admin` role.

Configuring Security in a Jakarta EE Application

Security configuration in Jakarta EE can vary depending on the environment and specific needs. However, basic configurations include the use of `web.xml` to specify security constraints and server configuration files, such as `domain.xml` for GlassFish or `standalone.xml` for WildFly.

1. **Security Configuration for the Application Server**:

To configure security in an application server like WildFly, you need to define security domains and user credentials.

Example configuration in `standalone.xml` for WildFly:

```xml
<security-domains>
    <security-domain name="MyDomain">
        <authentication>
            <login-module code="org.jboss.security.auth.spi.DatabaseServerLoginModule" flag="required">
                <module-option
```

```
name="dsJndiName"
value="java:/jboss/datasources/ExampleDS"/>

                <module-option
name="principalsQuery" value="select
password from Users where username=?"/>

                <module-option
name="rolesQuery" value="select role from
Roles where username=?"/>

            </login-module>

        </authentication>

    </security-domain>

  </security-domains>
```

This configuration defines a security domain that uses a database-backed login module.

Role Management and Security Policies

Managing roles and security policies is crucial

for defining permissions and access control. Jakarta EE allows you to define roles and associate permissions with resources and methods.

1. **Defining Roles**:

Roles are defined in the `web.xml` file or via annotations. Here's how to define a role in `web.xml`:

```xml
<security-role>
    <role-name>admin</role-name>
</security-role>
```

2. **Role-Based Security Policies**:

You can define security policies that control access to resources based on user roles. For example, you can secure a servlet or an EJB to allow access only to users with specific roles.

Testing Jakarta EE Applications

Testing is a fundamental aspect of application development to ensure that the software works as expected and to identify potential issues before deployment. In Jakarta EE, testing can be divided into two main categories: **unit testing** and **integration testing**.

Unit Testing and Integration Testing

Unit Testing

Unit testing focuses on verifying the functionality of individual code units, such as methods or classes, in isolation from the rest of the system. Tools like JUnit are commonly used for this purpose.

1. **Unit Testing a CDI Bean with JUnit**:

```java
import org.junit.jupiter.api.Test;
import jakarta.inject.Inject;
import static org.junit.jupiter.api.Assertions.assertEquals;

public class GreetingServiceTest {

    @Inject
    private GreetingService greetingService;

    @Test
    public void testGreet() {
        String result =
```

```
greetingService.greet("John");
        assertEquals("Hello, John!", result);
    }
}
```

In this example, we test the `greet` method of the `GreetingService` bean. Note that dependency injection may require the use of an embedded CDI container like Weld.

Integration Testing

Integration testing verifies the interaction between different components of the application and their integration with external resources such as databases or servers. Arquillian is one of the main tools for integration testing in Jakarta EE.

1. **Integration Testing Example with

Arquillian**:

```java
import org.jboss.arquillian.container.test.api.Deployment;
import org.jboss.arquillian.junit5.ArquillianExtension;
import org.jboss.shrinkwrap.api.ShrinkWrap;
import org.jboss.shrinkwrap.api.spec.JavaArchive;
import org.junit.jupiter.api.Test;
import org.junit.jupiter.api.extension.ExtendWith;
import jakarta.inject.Inject;
import static org.junit.jupiter.api.Assertions.assertEquals;

@ExtendWith(ArquillianExtension.class)
```

```
public class OrderServiceIT {

    @Inject
    private OrderService orderService;

    @Deployment
    public static JavaArchive
createDeployment() {
        return
ShrinkWrap.create(JavaArchive.class)
                .addClass(OrderService.class)

.addAsManifestResource("beans.xml");
    }

    @Test
    public void testPlaceOrder() {
        orderService.placeOrder("Test Item");
        // Verify the behavior of the
```

OrderService

        // ...

    }

}

```

This example shows how to configure an integration test using Arquillian and ShrinkWrap to create an instance of the `OrderService` bean.

### Tools and Frameworks for Testing

1. **JUnit**: Unit testing framework for writing tests for Java code.

2. **Arquillian**: Integration testing framework that supports testing Jakarta EE components in containerized environments.

3. **Mockito**: Used for mocking objects and dependencies during unit testing.
```

Mocking and Simulating Jakarta EE Contexts

Mocking and **simulating** Jakarta EE contexts are essential techniques for testing components that rely on external resources or services.

Mocking Example with Mockito:

```java
import org.junit.jupiter.api.Test;
import org.mockito.InjectMocks;
import org.mockito.Mock;
import org.mockito.MockitoAnnotations;

import static org.mockito.Mockito.*;
import static org.junit.jupiter.api.Assertions.*;
```

```
public class PaymentServiceTest {

  @Mock
  private PaymentGateway paymentGateway;

  @InjectMocks
  private PaymentService paymentService;

  @Test
  public void testProcessPayment() {
    MockitoAnnotations.openMocks(this);

when(paymentGateway.processPayment(any
Double())).thenReturn(true);

    boolean result =
paymentService.processPayment(100.0);
    assertTrue(result);
```

    }

}
```

In this example, we use Mockito to mock the `PaymentGateway` and inject the mock into the `PaymentService` to test the `processPayment` method.

### Strategies for Testing REST Services

Testing REST services involves verifying HTTP requests, status codes, and response content. Tools like **REST-assured** can be used to test REST APIs declaratively.

#### Testing a REST Service with REST-assured Example:

```java

```
import io.restassured.RestAssured;
import io.restassured.response.Response;
import org.junit.jupiter.api.Test;

import static org.hamcrest.Matchers.*;

public class OrderResourceTest {

    @Test
    public void testGetOrder() {
        RestAssured.given()
                .when()
                .get("/orders/1")
                .then()
                .statusCode(200)
                .body("id", equalTo(1))
                .body("status",
 equalTo("processed"));
```

```
    }
}
```

In this example, we use REST-assured to make a GET request to a REST service and verify the status code and response body.

Conclusion

Security and testing are crucial aspects of developing Jakarta EE applications. **Jakarta Security** provides the necessary mechanisms to ensure that applications are secure, managing authentication, authorization, and security policies. **Testing Jakarta EE applications

** ensures that the software is reliable and

functions as expected through unit and integration tests, using tools such as JUnit, Arquillian, and Mockito.

With a solid security configuration and an effective approach to testing, Jakarta EE applications can be developed and maintained with greater confidence in their integrity and robustness.

7.Deployment and Management of Applications

Packaging Jakarta EE applications involves creating distribution files that contain all necessary components for running the application on an application server. Jakarta EE applications can be packaged in various formats:

- **WAR (Web Application Archive)**: Contains web components such as servlets, JSPs, and configuration files. For example, `myapp.war` is a WAR file that includes all the web resources of the application.

- **EAR (Enterprise Archive)**: Contains multiple modules, including WAR files, JAR files, and shared libraries. For example, `myapp.ear` might include a WAR module for the web part and an EJB module for business logic.

- **JAR (Java Archive)**: Used for Enterprise JavaBeans (EJB) modules or shared libraries. For example, `myapp-ejb.jar` is a JAR file that contains EJB components.

Example of Packaging with Maven:

```xml
<build>
   <finalName>myapp</finalName>
   <plugins>
      <plugin>
         <groupId>org.apache.maven.plugins</groupId>
         <artifactId>maven-war-plugin</artifactId>
         <version>3.3.1</version>
         <configuration>
            <warSourceDirectory>src/main/webapp</war
```

```
SourceDirectory>
            </configuration>
        </plugin>
    </plugins>
</build>
```

This Maven configuration snippet sets up the WAR plugin to create a WAR file for deployment.

Deployment Strategies on Application Servers

Deploying a Jakarta EE application to an application server can be done through various methods:

1. **Manual Deployment**: Manual copying of the WAR or EAR file to the server's deploy

directory (e.g., `standalone/deployments` in WildFly).

2. **Automated Deployment**: Using tools like Maven or Gradle to automate deployment through specific plugins.

3. **Container Management**: Using Docker containers to create application images and deploy them to containerized environments like Kubernetes.

Example of Deployment with Maven:

```bash
mvn clean package
mvn wildfly:deploy
```

This command builds the WAR file and deploys it to a WildFly server using the WildFly Maven plugin.

Monitoring Running Applications

Monitoring running applications helps ensure that the application operates correctly and identifies potential issues. Common tools and techniques include:

- **JMX (Java Management Extensions)**: Allows monitoring and managing Java resources via MBeans.

- **Logging**: Using logging frameworks like Log4j or SLF4J to record events and issues.

- **Monitoring Tools**: Tools such as Prometheus and Grafana to collect and visualize application metrics.

Example of Logging Configuration:

```xml
<Configuration>
  <Appenders>
    <File name="FileLogger"
fileName="logs/app.log">
      <PatternLayout pattern="%d{yyyy-
MM-dd HH:mm:ss} %-5level %logger{36} -
%msg%n"/>
    </File>
  </Appenders>
  <Loggers>
    <Root level="info">
      <AppenderRef ref="FileLogger"/>
    </Root>
  </Loggers>
</Configuration>
```

This example configures a log appender to write messages to a log file.

Updates and Version Management

Managing versions and updates of applications can be achieved through:

1. **Semantic Versioning**: Using versioning conventions to facilitate version management of the application.

2. **Rolling Updates**: Implementing rolling updates or blue-green deployments to reduce risks associated with updates.

3. **CI/CD Tools**: Using Continuous Integration and Continuous Deployment tools like Jenkins to automate the build and deployment process.

Example of Semantic Versioning:

The version `1.2.3` represents:

- `1`: Major version (incompatible changes)
- `2`: Minor version (compatible feature additions)
- `3`: Patch version (bug fixes)

Best Practices and Design Patterns

Best Practices for Jakarta EE Development

1. **Separation of Concerns**: Use clear separation between presentation, business logic, and persistence to keep the code organized and manageable.

2. **Dependency Injection**: Prefer dependency injection over manual instantiation to improve modularity and testability.

3. **Error Handling**: Implement robust error handling and use logging mechanisms to facilitate debugging and maintenance.

4. **Use of Transactions**: Leverage Jakarta EE's transaction support to manage operations involving multiple resources securely and consistently.

Example of Using CDI for Dependency Injection:

```java
import jakarta.inject.Inject;

public class UserService {
```

```
    @Inject
    private UserRepository userRepository;

    public User findUserById(Long id) {
        return userRepository.findById(id);
    }
}
```

Common Design Patterns in Jakarta EE

1. **DAO (Data Access Object)**: A pattern for separating data access logic from the rest of the application.

2. **Service Layer**: A pattern for organizing business logic in a layer separate from controllers and repositories.

3. **Session Bean**: Use session beans to manage business logic and maintain application state.

Example of DAO Pattern:

```java
import jakarta.persistence.EntityManager;
import jakarta.persistence.PersistenceContext;

public class UserDAO {

    @PersistenceContext
    private EntityManager entityManager;

    public User findById(Long id) {
        return entityManager.find(User.class, id);
    }
```

}
```

### Performance Optimization

1. **Caching**: Implement caching to reduce the load on databases and improve response times.

2. **Connection Pooling**: Use connection pooling to optimize database access and reduce connection times.

3. **Profiling and Analysis**: Use profiling tools to identify and optimize performance bottlenecks.

**Example of Caching Configuration**:

```xml

```
<cache-container name="default">
   <local-cache-cache-container
name="myCache">
      <expiration max-idle="60000"/>
   </local-cache-cache-container>
</cache-container>
```

This example configures a cache container with an expiration setting for local cache.

8.Jakarta EE Glossary

Jakarta EE is a robust platform for developing enterprise applications in Java. To fully understand Jakarta EE, it's useful to become familiar with its specific vocabulary. This glossary covers key terms and concepts associated with Jakarta EE.

A

- **Annotation**: In Java, an annotation is a form of metadata that provides information to the compiler and runtime. In Jakarta EE, annotations are used to configure and manage components like EJB, CDI, and JPA.

- **Application Server**: Software that provides a runtime environment for web and enterprise applications. Examples include WildFly, Payara, and Apache TomEE.

- **Aspect-Oriented Programming (AOP)**: A programming paradigm that allows modularizing cross-cutting concerns, such as transaction management and security, by separating them from the main business logic. Jakarta EE does not include native AOP but frameworks like AspectJ can be used alongside it.

B

- **Bean**: In Jakarta EE, a bean is a software component that can be managed and used by a Jakarta EE container. Different types of beans include CDI Beans, EJB (Enterprise JavaBeans), and Managed Beans.

- **Bean Validation**: A Jakarta EE framework used to validate bean properties through annotations. It ensures that data meets certain constraints before being persisted or processed.

C

- **Contexts and Dependency Injection (CDI)**: A Jakarta EE specification that provides a framework for dependency injection and context management. It manages the lifecycle of beans and injection of services in a declarative way.

- **Container-Managed Persistence (CMP)**: A persistence mechanism that allows containers to manage data persistence for EJBs, reducing boilerplate code for database operations.

D

- **Dependency Injection (DI)**: A design pattern that allows dependencies to be passed to a component rather than having the component manage them itself. Jakarta EE uses DI to inject resources, services, and components into each other.

- **Deployment Descriptor**: An XML file that describes the configurations of a web or enterprise application. Files such as `web.xml` and `ejb-jar.xml` are examples of deployment descriptors in Jakarta EE.

E

- **Enterprise JavaBeans (EJB)**: Server-side components that encapsulate business logic and are managed by the EJB container. EJBs can be of three types: session beans, entity beans, and message-driven beans.

- **Entity Bean**: A type of EJB that represents a persistent entity in a database. Entity beans are used to manage data persistence and relationships between entities.

F

- **Facelets**: A view technology in Jakarta EE that replaces JSP (JavaServer Pages) for creating user interfaces. Facelets is mainly used with JavaServer Faces (JSF).

- **Facade Pattern**: A design pattern that provides a simplified interface to a complex system. In Jakarta EE, facades are often used to expose business services or EJB components in a straightforward manner.

J

- **JavaServer Faces (JSF)**: A component-based framework for building user interfaces. JSF is used to create MVC (Model-View-Controller) web applications in Jakarta EE.

- **Java Persistence API (JPA)**: An API for managing persistence and CRUD (Create, Read, Update, Delete) operations on Java entities. JPA provides a standard interface for working with relational databases in Jakarta

EE.

- **Java API for RESTful Web Services (JAX-RS)**: An API for creating RESTful web services in Jakarta EE. JAX-RS provides the annotations and classes needed to build and manage REST APIs.

M

- **Managed Bean**: A bean managed by the Jakarta EE container. Managed Beans can be used for presentation logic and integration with other application components.

- **Message-Driven Bean**: A type of EJB designed to process messages from a message queue or topic. Message-driven beans are used to integrate applications with messaging systems.

P

- **Persistence Context**: A JPA working session that manages a set of entities. The persistence context ensures that entities are managed and synchronized with the database.

- **Pooling**: A technique to optimize resource usage by creating and maintaining a pool of reusable objects, such as database connections or threads, to improve performance and reduce overhead.

R

- **Resource Injection**: The process by which the Jakarta EE container injects resources (such as database connections, JMS queues, or EJBs) into application components.

- **RESTful Web Services**: Web services that follow the REST (Representational State Transfer) architectural style, used to create scalable and interoperable APIs.

S

- **Session Bean**: A type of EJB that manages business logic and user session state. There are two main types of session beans: stateful (maintains state between calls) and stateless (does not maintain state).

- **Servlet**: A server-side component in Jakarta EE that handles HTTP requests and responses. Servlets are used to create dynamic content in web applications.

T

- **Transaction Management**: The process of managing transactions to ensure that database operations are atomic, consistent, isolated, and durable (ACID). Jakarta EE supports both declarative and programmatic transaction management.

- **Transaction Attribute**: Settings that define how a transaction should be managed in EJB, such as REQUIRED, REQUIRES_NEW, or MANDATORY.

W

- **Web Application Archive (WAR)**: A distribution file that contains all the necessary files for a web application, including servlets, JSPs, and configuration files.

- **Web Service**: An application that provides services via standard protocols like SOAP (Simple Object Access Protocol) or REST (Representational State Transfer). Jakarta EE supports both SOAP web services via JAX-WS and REST services via JAX-RS.

Z

- **Zero-Cost Abstraction**: A concept that involves using abstractions without introducing significant overhead compared to programming without abstractions. Jakarta EE aims to balance abstraction and performance to provide a powerful yet efficient framework.

This glossary provides an overview of key Jakarta EE terms and their applications. Understanding these concepts is essential for working effectively with Jakarta EE and developing robust, scalable enterprise applications.

Index

www.ingramcontent.com/pod-product-compliance
Lightning Source LLC
Chambersburg PA
CBHW052209220526
45471CB00004B/1885